PURSUING REDEMPTION

Life After Incarceration

By

MICHAEL A DAVIS

ISBN-10: 9798666400678

Contents

CHAPTER ONE

Seeking Change

Many individuals return home with the mindset to do right. The sad thing is that many often struggle due to the difficulties of securing housing and employment. Many of them are returning home with mental illnesses. An illness that may have went untreated while incarcerated. Only a small number are truly prepared for release, while the rest struggle to adjust when released.

Our criminal justice system has failed us for a long time. It continues to lack in resources, and this prevents individuals from being successful. When individuals are unable to find employment, they often turn to illegal activities to make money. Having no money coming in and bills are due, you usually do what you have to do to survive.

One common issue many face after incarceration is the lack of support. Many individuals coming home from prison need help, such as drug and alcohol treatment, mental health treatment. Most of them are unable to afford treatment. So they usually go without the treatment they need.

No, person should suffer because they can't afford the treatment they need. Someone who's been gone for an extended period might find it hard to adjust to a world that has changed overtime. A person who has been away for more than a few years will have difficulties navigating a world that has changed.

A person could emerge feeling vulnerable after being gone so long. Once out they will be met with many barriers. That includes housing and employment, when looking for employment or housing, their past often prevents them from advancing. Individuals will without doubt experience prejudice as a formerly incarcerated person.

Even after leaving prison, it can still feel like you are still in prison. It's true that once you have an x on your back, it will follow you around a lifetime. These rejections and consistent disrespect from society can lead to depression, and ultimately a loss of hope. It can be frustrating when you are trying to do right, but all you receive in return is rejection.

Working toward finding housing and employment with a record is no easy task, and it's something that everyone leaving prison goes through. It's not impossible, but will be challenging, it's something you have to be willing to work hard at. As we all know the system is not our friend, they want us to fail. That's why it is essential to prepare for your release on day one.

If the system is not willing to do it, then take it upon yourself to be ready mentally, physically, and spiritually to be successful. It is essential to prepare yourself for rejection. One thing you have to know is that dislike will be all around. Even family, friends, employers, and people in the community will reject you. But don't let that stop you from doing what you want.

It's all a part of the stigma that comes with being a felon. Learning to accept these rejections is going to be hard. But you have to take them as they go and keep living your life. No matter what past mistakes you made that led you to prison. Know that things will get better if you willing to put in the work.

Remember, you are not a failure, but a person who made some bad choices in life. We live and learn from mistakes. Don't get caught up in worrying about your mistakes. Resisting the negative influences will give you a better chance at success. No matter what you do, there's always someone trying to break you down. Never allow yourself to fall prey to those around you.

My advice would be to stay away from the negative vibe. Instead, surround yourself with people who want to see you make it in life. Find yourself with individuals who are involved with some sort of a faith-based group. Even connect with those who want to see you make it.

If they not motivating you to do right then they not the ones you should be around. The first few days to months will be a big challenge, so you need someone helpful in your corner. Let me be clear some family and friends. Will be willing to help you more than the rest. Those the ones you need to lean more toward.

It want be hard to spot those who want the best for you. The most important thing to remember is only you can define your future not no one else. That's why it is essential to be prepared to look for work upon release. Be willing to put in long hours searching for a job.

Even though it will be hard, you want to show them that you are looking for work. I know, and you know that you can't make a person give you a job. All you can do is try if you are able become your own boss. But for most that's not an option. As a formerly incarcerated person, you will fare poorly in the job market.

I am not trying to bring race into this, but we all knows that it's true. If you are of color, the job market will judge you harder. Being black or brown and a felon will put a double strain on you finding work. We will always have to work twice as hard; to them, we are a threat.

It's a fact that people of non-color have a better chance of getting employment with a record than those of color. Race can be more significant than a background check. That even include getting a callback for a second interview. A white person with a background has a better chance of getting a job, then some of the color without a criminal record.

Most people look at people of color as criminals, even if they never committed a crime in their lives. As a person of color, you are already living a life of double barriers; first, we have to deal with our high incarceration rate. We have to overcome racial discrimination in our everyday life.

Even the most qualified black man has it hard when trying to find a job. Many will live a life hampered permanently. Due to their criminal record, and those who do get hired suffer inequality in the workplace. Even those returning home deserve a stable job for the same reasons everyone else does. It's essential for those coming home to be employed so they can gain economic stability.

Just like I said before, having a job will reduce the likelihood of returning to prison. Not only that, it also promotes excellent public safety, and in the long run, everyone benefits from it. So, instead of shutting us out the labor market should embrace us.

It's no mystery that the job market for those coming out of prison is weak; one reason is fear of hiring someone fresh out of jail or prison. The concern is even higher if you are a person of color. The truth is that people fear to work with someone who has been to prison.

They believe that those arrested are all terrible persons, but that's far from the truth. Many of those returning home want to work and not be judge by their past. Yet, the world we live in does not see it that way. Discrimination against the formerly incarcerated will continue to happen. That's why we have to work hard and change the way they view us.

That's why we have to continue to network with those in a position to help us, such as job coaches, employment specialists, and life coaches. The list goes on it's many out there who want to help. Often, when formerly incarcerated individuals do find a job.

They are typically low-paying positions with no growth to advance. Due to the many barriers, we remain restricted to the type of jobs we can work. Some of those jobs are finance, health care, government, or even public education, just naming a few.

Depending on the nature of the crime or conviction, you can't hold specific occupational licenses. This rule will vary depending on the laws in your state. What people have to remember many of us want to work. But the thing is not many companies are willing to take a chance on someone who been to prison.

Some ideal jobs for those with a background are computer programmers, cooks, truck drivers, and construction, just naming a few. These are well-paying jobs for anyone coming home looking for a job. State laws strongly regulate many occupations. They do not believe that we should be able to achieve certain types of licenses.

That brings us to why so many employers are so hard-up hiring anyone with a background. It has to do with trying to keep their workplace safe. Also, they don't want to have any legal liability from the harm some may erupt. They feel like they are keeping their employees safe by not hiring us.

They look at hiring a formerly incarcerated individual as a risk to the company and its workers. But in fact, they are suffering from a misplaced fear of those who have been to prison. They fear hiring anyone with a background—a result of not realizing the negative impact of bias against ex-felons.

These companies' stereotypes hold many people with a record back from getting ahead in life. It has remained argued for years that providing stable employment to formerly incarcerated people helps them make a decent living and is more likely to keep them out of trouble. It will serve as a double win; we are happy, and the public is a little safer.

Rejecting an individual solely on the bias of a criminal record is poor practice. Many states are starting to ban the box on an employment form, which would prevent employers from asking about a criminal conviction on an application. Many places already prevent employers from asking about criminal records unless it is related to the job position.

Other laws make employees check for the accuracy of arrest and conviction. States need to enact laws that will forbid companies from disqualifying individuals solely on their background bias, unless the jobs deal with kids, the elderly, or the medical field and law enforcement.

I do agree that some areas need a background check, but not all jobs should solely base their hiring process on a background check. People change over time and should not be judge on past mistakes. Even with a background, it can be challenging for an employer to turn you away when you have the skills they want.

It is also true when the skills you have are in short supply. Therefore, going to a trade school to learn a trade is often key to securing a job in the field that you studied. Not only that, with the knowledge you learn in school, you can quickly own your own.

Even with a background, you can still be eligible for financial aid to cover the training cost. The thing that will most likely prevent you from getting financial assistance is being incarcerated at the time of applying or having drug-related convictions.

So, stay active and show prospective employers that you are a strong candidate. Let them know you have a strong work ethic and determination to succeed and advance with the company. One thing you could do is try and volunteer some time with local non-profits, which is a way for you to gain experience.

That way you can build up some trust with people in the community. It is an excellent way for you to gain some professional connections. The connections you gain can lead you to future job references. That alone can open the door for a better opportunity moving forward.

If you have skills that can lead you to be self-employed, go for it. By going that route, you can set yourself up to be an employee or business owner. The one thing to remember always be honest and don't try to cut corners. But never share more than you must. It's never good to lie about your past, but don't volunteer to share your history if they don't ask.

Remember that sharing too much can hurt you. So, never be willing to say more than you need. For saying to much can always come back to hurt you. That why it is up to you to plan your strategy. Never wait for others if possible do it on your own. For those returning to society without a place to live.

give up hope if it's a will there is a way. I know it's a sad feeling to be leaving prison. Which on top of that you leaving without a place to go. A large number of those living on the streets are there due to their incarceration. We all know it's hard to be successful without a place to live.

Having a roof over your head plays a large part in being successful after incarceration. If we are unable to find a solution, our homelessness problem will get worse. Having a place to sleep is a necessity that is often not met. For many formerly incarcerated individuals, having a home is usually a dream out of reach.

Many depend on others for a place to live. This elusive necessity, combined with other discriminations, makes it hard to survive life after incarceration. Before these individuals can deal with looking for a job or learning new skills, they need to secure housing sooner rather than later.

But because most places are unwilling to rent to anyone with a record, it can be hard to find a decent place to live. Most will likely find housing at a local homeless shelter which most centers limit how long you can be there. Some other options are living in a halfway or a sober living house, but even these places cost money, and they come with many pros and cons.

One thing I can say is: living in these places; there's never a dull moment. The good thing about these places, you are in an environment where you can related to those around you. Everyone here is basically going through the same problems. These places can often assist you with different types of resources; although, these places can be hard on someone coming straight out of prison.

I'm sure all these places have strict rules and breaking any of those rules can result in the program's booting you out. If you are on parole, that could be a violation. These homes often make you accountable for all your actions. Those who are just coming home can benefit from having somebody supervise their behavior.

Taking this direction is not always the right option for everyone. For most, it's either this option or return to your old environment, and most likely, that environment is what got you in trouble. If you have a past addiction, it is best to try going to a sober living home.

If you want to build a new foundation on a clean slate, it's best to seek recovery. Living in a place like a halfway house means that you live under set rules and guidelines. Some of those rules are having a curfew, drug testing, and classes to attend daily. For most, having a structure is a good thing, especially those seeking recovery need this type of guidance.

If you want to beat your addiction, then going to a facility like this will be in your best interest. When going to these programs, know that you have to be self-motivated to complete the program. Some programs can take months to finish, while some programs require you to be in the program for up to a year.

But don't let my opinions deter you from going. I'm just here to share what I know and what I have heard about these places with you. A lot of these facilities are not able to treat the psychological aspects of addiction. Don't limit yourself to resources many outside program are able to help you as well.

These programs would most likely be able to guide you on where to go for help. If you are not dealing with addiction and need a place to live, you may want to look at boarding houses for the time being. These places allow you to be more independent; you are pretty much on your own in these places.

In a boarding house, you buy your food and prepare your meals. Here, you will meet many different people, and you can expect most to be always coming and going. You will see different types of people, and you will like some and dislike others. You will have to prepare for that, but you will need employment to live in one of these places.

When living in a boarding house, you will have to learn how to live on a budget. Try buying only the things you need from month to month. So, you have to be wise when it comes to spending your money. I know you don't plan on living there forever, so it's best to put your money into a savings account.

That way, you are not overspending, and you can better manage your money when you can't get to it. Your main goal needs to be seeking employment if you are not currently working. You also need to seek a more suitable living environment. Choosing to live at a halfway house can benefit you; these homes are for those who would otherwise remain detained.

While living in a halfway house, you will most likely set your mind on being there for the shortest possible time. Sometimes your stay can inadvertently last up to one year, but these places will help you learn the skills needed to reenter society. Living here gives you time to get on your feet, get a steady job, and feel secure.

People who often go to these institutions are those who suffer from mental or physical disabilities. The good thing about a halfway house is, they can provide many resources. These residences can receive the right skills that will enable them to better support themselves.

The facilities are more flexible with helping you get medical and psychiatric help and even social services. The purpose of being in a halfway house is to go through reintegrating seamlessly into society. These facilities help people transition back into the community under supervision. Outside of these places, some other options you can try our local homeless shelters.

The Salvation Army will be able to assist you with a case manager. They often offer the best services and results if you have no other options. It's not the best, but they are better than nothing. Salvation Army has helped individuals coming home from prison.

When an individual receives the right tool to succeed, the outcome will always be on the right side. Salvation Army provides a program that has been successful for years. Their pathway program ensures that their client is less likely to re-offend. The Salvation Army provides everyone in their program with an advisor who develops a plan to address your personal needs.

Both of you sit together, discuss, and create a goal that will lead you to success. Not only that, you also receive spiritual development as well as counseling. They give you the option to receive both educational and job readiness skills. Those in need of substance or mental health support can receive that service. Many already know of Salvation Army because of their services inside of prison.

One other place where you can seek help is at goodwill. They offer many services to those returning home. The pay is not well but goodwill provide many jobs for those returning home. These jobs can be in their stores or warehouses. They offer many programs that those coming home can benefit from. But just like any program they only work if you allow them to work.

For what I have experience they do provide effective services. What I learned is be willing to make the program work in your favor. Any resource available to you take it. The more help you can get the better off you will be. Goodwill reentry programs are structured for you to succeed if you are willing to do the work.

CHAPTER TWO

Succeeding

Yes, after you return home things will be difficult. There will be many obstacles to overcome. First do remember that you are in control of your destiny. Life will be what you make it; either you will succeed, or you will fail. To survive after release, you have to remain focused and keep a clear mind.

Staying away from negative influences will play a significant role in your reentry. The main thing you have to do is build confidence in yourself. Having confidence in yourself will be key to surviving. The one important thing you need is to build a network. A network of people who are in position to help you be successful.

Make sure these people will have a positive influence on you upon your reentry. Having positive people around you will help shield off malicious individuals. During this time, you have to be determined if you want to succeed. Don't rushing into something because it sounds good.

Always do your research before making life changing decisions. During this new beginning be inspired. Not inspired in others, but in yourself to be the change you want to be. This transition will not be easy, and life will hand you some curveballs.

Don't let those disappointments stress you out. Stay positive and stay on the path to success. Do something that you have passion for. If you have yet to discover what your passion is, then go out and find it. Let your love be what makes you motivated going forward. What you do from this point onwards will define who you are.

So, go out into the world and work hard, live life to the fullest and enjoy every moment. Getting involved in your community will help you to adjust to society. Joining a social group is an excellent way to show that you want better in life. Some people will help you every step of the way. They are the ones who will understand you.

They will be able to guide you in the right direction. Not only are you networking but you are creating a bond. Being involved in a group allows you to bond well with others. Not only that it also help you to create a friendship that can last a lifetime. In addition to that it add another level of accountability.

It will be beneficial for you when transition back into society. Those individuals will be the ones who can help you in many ways. The support of a group of people who have experienced prison will be decisive. A social group is a place where you can go and not be judged based on your past.

These are people who have been through what you are going through now. So, they will be an excellent asset to your success. It would help if you had a plan and a goal drafted once you are released. During this time you have to keep a positive attitude. Having a negative behavior only lead to failure and destruction.

Because of your record life will test you; things want be easy so stay motivated. When you having a bad day let it be motivation to make it through. The darkest part of your life is over. Today is the day you focus on the positive things in life. No matter how much you prepare for your release, it will never be enough. To be successful after incarceration you need to let go of criminal ways. If you are not ready, then prepare yourself for a return to prison. If you are like me, then I know you want to change and stay out of trouble. It's not hard to do right; you have to have the mindset to do right.

Family and friends will be necessary during this time as they will play a big part in your overall success. If you don't have any, then reach out to a church or social group; they will assist you. Do not let pride stand in your way of succeeding. There will be people who are going to judge you solely on your past. Never let anyone stop you from reaching your goals.

If they for you then they are against you. In life you will be faced with adversity. But the test comes when dealing with that adversity. Go out there and prove them all wrong. Don't just be another number. Be someone who got out and did something in life. Go out there and show them that you want to be a productive member of society.

If you want the stigma to change, then it's up to you to make it happen. With all the obstacles to overcome, some of your biggest downfalls can come from family, friends, and loved ones. So, choose whom you want to entertain. Not everyone want you to succeed; there will be people who want to see you fail.

Don't be one of those scared to ask for help; many people fail because they were too afraid to ask for help. We will face many challenges in life, but we face those challenges in the quest for a better tomorrow.

Many problems can either make or break you. Along with these challenges we gain wisdom.

If you are afraid of challenges, then you will never know your full potential. Each challenge will build your strength and character. The best thing about a challenge is overcoming what they say you cannot. Do not let a challenge become an obstacle; being successful after prison is possible. To be successful after release, you must learn how to train your mind.

Training your mind is the first step to success. While education is the core process of gaining knowledge. Just picking up a book at a local library can benefit your future. If you can believe and dream it, then nothing stopping you from achieving it? So, be prepared for a new beginning, be prepared to conquer your fear of failure, and let down.

Remember that nothing happens overnight. Every moment that you are out is a moment in your new beginning. Surprisingly, little is impossible for the human mind, and we can do almost anything we put our minds on. Creativity is given to us all, so what creativity can you share with the world?

I learned that you could make your most cherished dream possible by doing what's necessary at the moment. Remember when one door closes, the next door opens; each entry can lead you to bigger and better things, and you just have to prepare yourself for the journey that awaits you.

Don't be one of those who get stuck looking at the locked door, not realizing the door ahead is unlocked. Know that there are more positive things around you in the distance. You just have to be willing to go out and find it. Some days, it may be hard to see the positive in life because our society is toxic.

You are going to have to look harder on some days to see the positive. Many of you have failed over and over in life, and that's ok. The thing is, learning from your failure will make you succeed if you continue to fight for it. During your darkest moments, you have to keep it together and focus on the light ahead.

Most of our outcome in life is out of our control. What you do have control over is the effort you put into it. In life, you have to remember that life is not about material things; it's about what you learned and what you could teach the next person. It's not always about what you can do for yourself but what you can do for someone else.

When you can help the next person in need, good things happen in return. Show them that you are a product of your own decision. Once you develop hope, then the sky is the limit for you. The best preparation in life is to do your best every day. If you can change your way of thinking, then you can change your way of living.

The options you have with a felony compared to those without a felony are different. That's why it's important not to lose hope. So many people have found success after incarceration. If you want a success story start working toward that goal. Nothing good comes easy, and if you want it, be ready to work hard for it.

The most important thing is staying out of trouble and away from those involved in the drama. Many of us are not the same individuals we once were. Many of us genuinely do want to change and be better people. We need the community to believe in us. We need the community to get behind us, we all know it's only a few out there willing to support us.

It's hard starting over once you return home, especially when you don't have a support system to get you through the uncertain times. Many individuals don't know how to start over after serving a long stretch in prison. Given, it can become overwhelming at first, especially when you don't know what to expect.

So many individuals return to jail because the challenges were too enormous for them to overcome. That is why it is essential to find reentry programs or support groups to help you. These programs or groups can be critical to someone who has been gone for a long time. The groups and programs are where you will find the most compassionate people.

Those who know and understand what you are going through. Being sympathetic to someone helps them reenter society and gives them hope to fight for a better tomorrow. It doesn't mean that you are excusing them from their past behavior. But it does let them know that things will be ok.

By showing individuals compassion, you help them gain confidence, making individuals coming home to be more effective in life. As formerly incarcerated individuals, we have it hard to survive in a world that continues to condemn us. Many individuals return to prison after release for a short time due to the lack of support after returning home.

Despite the second chance act of 2005, we still face many challenges. The number one reason we often fail to reintegrate is the lack of preparation before leaving prison. You need to get those first few days right because it will be harder to get the rest right if you don't. What you do on day one will define if you make it.

Don't be one of those who get released and end up at the club that night. That will lead you to go back to doing what landed you in jail in the first place. There will be time later down the road to go out and have fun. But at the moment, you need to be about your business. I have seen it happen multiple times.

I'm not telling you not to have fun, but those first few days need to go toward being productive. Those few days after release will be tough; you need to be prepared mentally for what the world will throw at you. After your discharge, you must surround yourself with people who are grounded. So, don't be quick to jump into a relationship.

That will be a mistake if you are coming home single. I know you want companionship, but it's best to wait until you're stable. Don't think you can make it on the outside as you did on the inside. The anger you had on the inside want work in the real world if you're going to make it.

The prison world and the free world are two different worlds, so you have to adjust to this world as you will end up back where you don't want to be. Although the choices you make will be on you, at some point, you have to humble yourself, or the system will humiliate you. The world, as you remember, it has profoundly changed, from technology to fashion trends.

The world didn't stand still while you did your time, and when you are released, you will find yourself playing catch up. You will realize that technology has improved, and our criminal justice system has changed. It will be difficult for you to adjust to it. It's going to be a shock at first, but you will learn to adjust to the changes as time goes on.

CHAPTER THREE

Never Give Up

Now that you free understand that you can't make up for the lost time. It's time to go out and find your place; it's time for you to find your purpose. While out searching don't forget to have some perseverance. Don't allow someone else's passion to be your passion. Instead, go out and discover your power. Don't be afraid to fail while trying to find your purpose.

Every great person have fail at something in life. Failing is about learning from your failures. You have to be confident in yourself at some point, and you have to want more out of life. The little things you learned in prison should've changed your perception of life. Don't feel like just because you served some time, you can't be successful.

Remember that just because you been to prison. Don't mean you can't get out and still have a successful life. The only difference is they went out and did things the right way. If you have the heart and believe in yourself you can do anything. Take a moment and reflect on your past and where you want to be.

Being lazy and having egotistical thinking will prevent you from making effective decisions. We can only do what we can. Learning to accept who you are and what you lack is all you need to push forward. I learned that I had to grow comfortable with my flaws while learning to love myself. Once you do that then you gain confidence in yourself.

Never wait for someone to give you validation. The only validation you need is your own. Make the best out of every situation you face in life, no matter what the case may be. Sometimes it takes going through a negative experience to receive a positive experience. Going through negative and painful experiences will help you to mature and grow.

Once you accept failure as your lesson, you will be able to benefit from those failures. The sooner you can learn to control your character and whom you choose to entertain, the sooner you can move on from those who can't help you. If they can't add value or can't help you advance in life, cut them loose. There comes a time when you have to take a step back and breathe a little.

If you believe in what you are trying to accomplish, don't allow anyone to come between that. If you want to be a winner, then you have to keep a clear mind. Get ready and prepare for a battle. Trying to survive while seeking your purpose is not easy. If you continue to work hard at what you believe in, you will be successful.

I can't say this enough stress to you. The only acceptance of your past mistakes should be from self. Never look for others to accept you. At this point, they shouldn't even matter to you. Every life experience you face can either make you or break you. But the most important thing you can do is learn.

We have to have the ability to turn our negative into a positive. Every decision you make in life has consequences, and some of our choices can be hard. It's one of those things where you have to accept it and move on. You can't allow others to determine if you succeed or fail.

The decision you make not only hurt you. But those around you are affected as well. So, you have to come up with a plan and decide what steps you can take in order to safeguard yourself from failure. Every progress starts with the mind and it begins when you can change your pattern of thinking.

The only person who is capable of changing your life is you. You are the only person that can determine what you are willing to tolerate. Taking responsibility for your own choices is when you begin to grow and learn from your failure. When you fail, don't play the blame game. Critically examine the part you played in your defeat.

Taking responsibility for your choices is difficult to do. It takes courage to admit that you tried and failed. But it takes a wise person to learn from failure. We all are human, and we all screw up at times. That's a part of life we live and learn. We can achieve so much if we allow ourselves to want more in life. Never settle for less when you can have more.

We have to stop fighting with ourselves and start trusting in our life journey. If you are willing to listen to yourself, then you can find away. When you can be true to yourself, you can grow and take advantage of your journey. We hold the key to our future.To get to the future, you got to leave the past in the past.

When one door closes, another one opens. But it is up to you to define what the next entry will be. Continue to push forward and hope for the best; don't let fear cause you to fail. Again, don't get caught up worrying about everyone, that you forget about what you want out of life.

Never allow someone else to judge you because they are not perfect either. Don't let your downfall be their happiness. You can only live for yourself and no one else; what others think of you doesn't matter. Don't be afraid of making a mistake; just learn from those mistakes and move on.

Know that every move you make is essential when it comes to personal growth. Every step forward will get you one step closer to where you want to be. Sometimes even a lousy step is often the step we needed to take. It may be the step we need to set us on the right path. When you can get past the uncertainties, you will learn how to manage it.

I know what it like to feel the shame and guilt of past mistakes. These things often keep us from trying to progress forward positively. Remember the past is the past and you can't change it. So, why continue worry about the things you can change. At some point in life, you have to believe in yourself even when no one else does.

The time for change is now so out and own your destiny. Once you decide you want to succeed, give up on feeling sorry for yourself. Don't let your inner thoughts make you lose your blessings. I want to challenge you to start believing in you. Because if you don't believe in you, why should someone else believe in you.

Don't worry about anything else; forget about the things that won't help you grow. Don't let anything slow you down. Follow your heart and do what's best for you. The lesson is to stop overthinking and just let it happen. Listen to your heart and find the courage to follow your heart and go with the flow. When you follow your heart it will enable you to discover new things.

Once you can follow your heart, it will give you a newfound respect for yourself. That will allow you to focus on the things that matter the most. When you follow your heart, you will know if you are genuinely on the right path. Start focusing on the present and not the past. Don't worry about the future, for tomorrow is the unknown.

Worry about the present moment because it will define your future. No matter what you may be going through, love who you are. Accept the things you cannot change. Whatever you went through in the past happen for a reason. Know that each of those things made you stronger and taught you something useful.

It also gave you the drive to do better.

Whatever you did or went through made you wiser and gave you the motivation to keep fighting. As you know you should never give in to the naysayers. Many things in this world catch the human eye. But only a few things will capture the heart. Always believe in yourself, and never give up when things get hard.

When you can make peace in your heart, you will start to move in the right direction. Don't let anyone or anything stray you from what you want. Never wait on things to happen. Go out, and make things happen. The work you do now will define who you are later. Never settle for less when you can have more.

The good things in life are always hard to achieve. But those things that are bad is easy to achieve. So, do you want the easy way or the hard way? We have all had a taste of the easy way. Why not try the hard way. Only a few are willing to take the challenging route. Keep a clear mind and stay positive things will work if you allow them to work.

Go out and seek help there's nothing wrong with needing help. Having a little faith and confidence is enough to achieve the most difficult things. So let go of your worries relax and enjoy life. It's our most significant failures that we learn the most. Everything we do in life is a learning experience. Don't be afraid to attempt something new.

Don't be one of those people who live in regret of never trying. It's easier to live with failure than it is to live with never trying. Instead we should focus more on those chances we allow to pass us up. There's no point in having dreams or ideas if you are too afraid to pursue them.

CHAPTER FOUR

The Journey

As you venture into a new chapter of life, you will notice all around you that so much is changing. Each decision you make today will have an impact moving forward. As humans we reserve the ability to overcome our obstacles. As you do so, there will be many roadblocks on your journey; some are bad, and some will make you want to give up.

As you prepare for the adventures ahead, create new habits that will keep you moving forward. Those new habits should match your unique lifestyle. Create a vision that is compatible with your habits. In the beginning, things always seem complicated not be afraid just embrace change.

It's time you think about reinventing yourself. Don't let other's fears and burdens cause you hardship. Go out and rediscover what was once acceptable to your soul. Let go of those ghosts that's been haunting you. Above anything else, you have to value your own relationship with self. Get out a pen and pad and write down ways to change your lifestyle.

I would advise you to empty the trash. Let go of the things that don't serve a purpose. Innovate new ways of thinking and develop new strategies as well as new habits.

So, what modern masterpiece will you create? What is your new standard of living? From this day forward what can you do to be better.

What can you do to be success, many of you know what it's like to start over? Sometimes, we are face with many factors that force us to change in our life. Sometimes we need to take a risk to escape destructive behaviors. It's your time to show the world who you can be. Not only that what you can become in life.

As you go out and take on the world don't loss focus on what you want out of life. don't fall prey to thing that don't really matter at the time. What matter is you stay out trouble? It's always easy to get into but hard to get out of.

Today failure can open the door to a new opportunity. Each day you get up is a new opportunity and a fresh start in life. Every moment of our life is precious, and a gift so make the best of it. Just set back and be patient. This isn't something that will happen quick. But it will happen at the right moment.

When starting over things will not happen quickly, so you have to be patient. When you begin to explore a new chapter in life, it will come with many requirements.

You will have to learn how to have faith and courage. Not only that, you need inner strength, and most of all, you need self-love.

Most of all, you must come to terms that you are not a finished product. Our life wasn't meant to be comfortable, and that's why we live a life as a process of becoming. We go through so much to find ourselves and to become whom we want to be in life. Our life is about living and learning each day; it allows us to discover more about ourselves.

We have to be prepared to embrace change in our life. Learn to accept what is and surrender to it; you have to let it be at the end of the day. Accept the situation that you in, no matter how hard it may be. It's time you make peace with your present. Pray and ask for guidance during your journey. Be grateful, and don't worry about things.

Instead, let things play out. We often get caught up with worry about things that we can't control. Stop and be grateful for what you do have. Sometimes we have to be thankful for what life has given us. When you are grateful for what you have, you will end up having more than what you had.

If you are searching for something new on your journey, you have to give up everything from the past. Let go of your history, for the future holds many secrets waiting for you to discover them. Often, we have to trust in the wisdom of life, putting aside all doubts.

We have to let experience guide us and hope for a good outcome. When you put trust in life, you are allowing life to lead you in the right direction. If you ask God to lead you, He will lead the way. Let that be part of your daily thing to do. Ask for guidance and strength to find the right path. Ask Him to reveal to you how to live a healthier life.

We have to learn that we need to make peace with the idea that life is a journey. We have to start living life and not worry about things that won't help us advance. We have to get into the habit of appreciating every moment of our life. Each day that we wake up is another day of life. Embrace the moment because they are priceless.

I've learned that when starting fresh you have the power to put your past behind you. Going through change will be overly exciting for you. As you continue on this journey, prepare yourself for any challenges you may face. One thing to remember is that the good outweighs the bad. Every point in life tells a story, but it's up to on how your story to ends.

So, as you explore life differently, conduct a personal check sheet before you jump into a task. Allow yourself the ability to navigate your way through this with ease. When you get to the point where you are overwhelmed take it easy and relax. Allow yourself time to think the problem out.

The issues you face going forward are going to test you. Allow those issues to build up your strength and character. As you realize your journey will never be comfortable; remind yourself to choose a path that has a purpose. Make sure that it's a purpose that you can feel in your heart.

Always do what you think is right, not what you think is right. Always choose the path that is right for you. Not what someone else think is right for you. Now is the time to take control of your fate. I can't tell you personally where to find the courage; that part is up to you. But what I can tell you, when you have a moment where you are feeling down, can get back up.

Always meet your challenges head-on and give it you're all. I have endured so much like many of you. I've had my share of hardship, and I know what it's like to be lost and broken. One thing I will never forget is where I've been. But most of all, where I want to be.

As time goes by things always get easy. The things I went through and endured only made me stronger. Sometimes, it takes us to get knocked down for us to stand up more substantial. I say to you - go out and build your foundation. Throughout this journey, continue to grow and improve your way of living.

Even what you do not make others proud, be proud of yourself no matter what. When you do right, you will succeed. No matter what may come your way, don't let it overwhelm you. Always remember that mistakes will happen in life. We live, and we learn, and then we move on.

No matter how long it takes you to reach your destination, know that it will be worth it in the end. Each of us has our destiny in life. We will all be tested and challenged differently, but we have to have the will to survive until the end. Never have any regrets for anything you do in life.

Your journey is about you and you alone, don't depend on the next person to help you. Always be the best that you can be. Don't get wrapped up in your final destination that you forget to enjoy the ride this journey will take you on. So, buckle up, sit back, and enjoy the ride, for, at times, it will be bumpy.

Every So Often the choices we make in life are not always the right choice. Because we are not perfect, and we all make wrong decisions, no matter who you are. I have never met a perfect person; never once have I met someone who didn't make a mistake in life. The choices you make may not always be right. But that's ok because we are not perfect.

Don't get too caught up on yesterday that you forget about today. Today's gift gives us the ability to overcome the challenges of yesterday. Only you can define what will come of today, while tomorrow holds the unknown. You either stand for something or fall for anything. Don't wait until it is too late the time is now.

Sometime the best things in life are worth the wait. So I ask you do you have what it takes to make it to the finish line? Continue to fight, claw, slide, walk whatever it takes to make it there. We all have the potential of being great, but greatness doesn't come easy. It's something that takes time and hard work.

When trying to reach that level of greatness, you have to step outside of your comfort zone. Setting goals and sticking with them is the first step. When on the journey to excellence, you have to strive and work hard every day to be better. It's not easy; it's something that will take time and hard work.

Just because you have a record doesn't mean you can't be great. You have to be willing to take advantage of each and every opportunity. If you want to succeed, you have to stay focused. Never lose focus, because if you do, you will fail and fail hard.

Learn from them and build off of what they did. Now I'm not saying do it the same way. Because what worked for them may not work for you. Use what they did and build your blueprint and go from there. Don't get discouraged if others don't see your dream.

Many have been in your shoes, and many of them are thriving now. Like many have said in the past, the only impossible journey is the one you don't take. Success is not a destination but a journey we are trying to complete. Don't rush to get to the top. As fast as you got there, the quicker you can fall back down.

Achieving excellence takes time and dedication. Learns how to stop doing less and starts doing more. Never limit yourself to less when you can have more. Often, we sell ourselves short on the things we can do because we didn't think we could do more as we can go as far as our minds let us. Greatness lies in the right of strength.

Never allow someone to tell you what you can and can't do. Often, they do that to keep you from being more successful than them. You want to be able to prove those who doubted us wrong. No matter what others do or say, dreams can come true. Just have the courage to pursue those dreams.

When we learn to turn our obstacles into opportunities the sky becomes the limit. You are the only one who can overcome your obstacles; no one else can do it for you. If you want to be a winner, you have to learn how to become a winner. Those who are successful are successful because they refused to give up.

I don't know about you, but I'm not willing to give up. You can't achieve anything if you don't have hope, faith, and confidence in yourself. We have to learn how to go beyond failure and refuse anything less than success. The choice is yours; just make sure the choice you make is right.

As humans, we often struggle with this more often than you think.

We are all born with a purpose in life. No matter what that purpose maybe. The one thing to remember is to work hard to be good at it. Sometimes all we need is to reevaluate our life priorities. I recommend starting by working on it today. It's no secret that finding your purpose is no easy task, and it may take some time to discover.

If you haven't yet uncovered your intention, don't worry. It will come to you at the right moment. Everything we go through in life is part of a life lesson. We have to go through things to prepare us for our purpose. Obstacles are a part of our everyday growth process. Figure out what you want out of life.

Then, come up with a way to get it. We often give up because we don't know how to. We are here for a purpose. Instead of losing yourself to technology, take advantage of your downtime, talk with others, and read a book, do things that will build knowledge.

Go out and connect with those you often see. Build a relationship ask about themselves and what they do for a living. Ask if they love their job; you can even ask what their interests are passionate about. Most will be willing to share.

No matter who you are, we are all born with much potential to fulfill our life and career goals. You may find many things that you are good at doing. It's your job to find out what you are passionate about. Find the thing that has the most meaning to you. What are you most inspired about, and why? What is it that brings joy to your heart the most?

I don't know about you, but I know that I'm tired of working for others. I want to do something more with my life, something that is important. Get fed up with living life for others. It's time to start living for you. For the rest of your life, make it about discovering the things that make you happy. If you asked the question, "what makes you happy?" How would you answer that?

I don't know about you, but I'm tired of going to work without a purpose. I'm sick of working a job just to get by. No matter the job or the position. I know having a job is part of surviving. I know it has to be a better way. Living your purpose is every human destiny that we all want to achieve. Identify your real job, not what you do for money, but what you love to do to fulfill your purpose. With all the things going on in the world, we can sometimes get lost.

CHAPTER FIVE

Redemption

When I thank about redemption, I think of it as forgiving yourself and starting fresh. It's a way of leaving the past in the past while looking to the future. Redemption is not about being perfect; it's about making a change doing things a different way. No matter what you did in the past, you can change.

Redemption allows you to explore new opportunities and discover new things about yourself. There comes a time in life when we have to get over our shortcomings. We have to challenge ourselves to be better. Our pathway to redemption will be challenging but not impossible.

Accepting your wrong and moving on will give you peace. We have to make every effort to do better. Everyone is worthy of redemption you just have to want it. What about a formerly incarcerated individual? Do they deserve a second chance?

To be even more precise, do you think anyone who been on the inside deserves a second chance? The answer is yes because everyone makes mistakes. We are all humans and deserve to have a second chance at life. No matter how big or little the mistake is, we earned a chance to redeem our actions.

But many often face being judged their entire life, which can make their road to redemption a little challenging. Remember that it doesn't matter what you have done or who you are. Through the power of hard work, you will make it. Anything is possible if you believe and want it.

Know that better days are ahead, and if you genuinely want it, you have to work hard at it and not let anybody stop you. One of the most important things is having the ability to recover. Through God, you can recover. The word of God changes lives. No matter who you are and why you went to prison, you can change, and every person has dignity and the potential to change.

No matter what others may say, we are all deserving of a second chance at life. No matter what, never stop trying; never stop believing in what you can achieve. The one piece of advice I can give you is this; stay away from those who belittle you. We are all born to be winners, but you have to plan for it to be a winner.

So, go ahead, start preparing to be a winner, and don't accept anything less. Today is the beginning of something new; remember that everything happens for a reason, even though we often never know the reason why it happens. We have to realize that we have to make good on our opportunities.

Because if you don't, who knows if you will ever get that opportunity again. We have to remember that every day is a new day and another chance of being a better person. No matter what others may tell you, your dreams are not a waste. You are good enough to do and be whatever you want to be in life.

Remember that many of us have to go through the storm to see the sunshine. Yes, there will be times when you feel like life is kicking your butt. There will be times when you feel as if you can't keep going. Realize that you have already been to the bottom, and the only way to go is up from here. What you are going through now will surely pass.

Everything will be ok. Just continue to fight until you win the war. To those of you that are struggling with redemption, hold on to hope. Hold on to your dreams and keep pushing, for the sky is the limit. Yes, you will fail at times, but know that with failure, there is a success.

We are all humans, and no matter what, we all stumble in life. So, when you do stumble, pick yourself up, and keep pushing. The most important thing to remember is that you have to keep faith in yourself. Never doubt yourself or your abilities to be whatever you want to be in life.

Know that you will develop and grow and achieve many great things. As long as you stay true to yourself, nothing else matters. We all are capable of doing beautiful things. I hope these words encourage you as you go forward with life. Remember this one thing; only you hold the key to your future.

Only you can define what your future will be. I hope you make the right decisions, and I hope that all the choices you make will be the right ones. What you do going forward will not only affect you but those around you. I'm confident that you will lead by experience.

For those of you who are struggling, believe in your ability to do right. Go out there and take on the world head-on. Each of you who reads this book can prove your doubters wrong. Each of you has the mindset to demonstrate your true potential to change your way of life. People deserve the right to a second chance, but it is up to you to make fair use of that chance.

I, for one, know that it won't be easy. But it is possible if you want it bad enough, so the question is; how bad do you like it? There are many doubters out there who don't believe in second chances. So, prove them wrong. When you think about making a change in your life, you have to embrace it fully.

You have to be willing to try new things without fear of failure. Failure is something that will always be a part of our life. As a human, you have to learn how to get over that failure and learn from it. We have to live life to its full capacity no matter what.

Why does anyone want to stay in the same place without ever experiencing change? If you love something enough, you will change. We all can change our actions. Stop waiting for others to come and rescue you. Instead, save yourself. All we can do is move on and do better. Change only happens if you put effort into changing.

Change is something that you have to do on your own. Never change for someone else's pleasure; do it for you. Do it because it is the right thing to do if you want better in life. Then you are going to have to make a change. The environment you choose to be in will a lot.

To change you have to be in a good atmosphere. If you don't choose the right, you will most likely fail. Sometimes, you have to improve your habits, and by doing that, you have to look at yourself. If you are hoping for a specific outcome, you have to do what is needed to complete your goal. Putting yourself in a positive environment will set you on the right path.

Set yourself up for success, you have to be motivated to be successful. Learn how to have the mindset to make better decisions. Train your mind to practice better habits. When you can turn your negative to a positive, you will make better choices. We all have goals that we want to achieve.

But we can't achieve those goals if we don't do what is right. If we try doing things the wrong way, we know what the outcome could be. Staying in a toxic environment can cost you everything. So, that's why it is crucial to choose your company wisely.

Do not expect others to change around you; be the one who is doing the changing. The key ingredient to change begins with you. You have to lead by example; don't wait on others to change. If you are trying to be an influence on others, you have to influence yourself first. Learn how to develop the will to trust your actions.

When you can lead by example, your efforts will show, and it will serve you in the right way. Our efforts can help others to see and accomplish their own goals. If you are aiming to change others, make sure that you are changing as well.

I will say that don't let other people's negative feedback shift your thinking toward malicious behavior. Instead, prove them wrong by doing what they say you can't do. I know better than anyone that negative feedback does not feel right, no matter who gives it. We all would rather have positive feedback any day of the week.

Sometimes, we need that negative feedback, mostly because we need to feel uncomfortable sometimes. There is no way to avoid change; it's something that is part of our life. It is our choice if we want positive change or negative change. Our positive change can have an impact on others to change.

Don't allow your dreams to become hidden; instead, set goals that will enable you to achieve those dreams. Let go of regrets instead, decide how you want to do better. Make the change now before it is too late. If you're going to overcome your fears, you have to be willing to soar higher.

Don't be one of those people who only watch others soar and stand there, looking and wondering if you can do it or not. You have to be willing to leap if you want to fly high. No dream is too big to achieve. Do not live life to exist; at some point in life, you have to try.

Why work at something you hate when you can work somewhere that you love. If you decide to leap, know that you will take some bumps and bruises. Don't let the fear of failure stop you from jumping. If you want to be successful, you have to leap; success doesn't come if you don't try first.

When you jump, don't be afraid to fail. Failure is a part of growing and learning that is a part of life. We are all created with a gift; no one is born without a gift. There's no easy road to success without hard work. Every one of us is a work in progress. It may be hard in the present, but best believe it will all be worth it in the end.

Whatever your passion is, don't ignore it, and don't let anyone lead you away from that passion. Don't get caught up in living for others dream. Don't let another person's dream keep you from your imagination. Don't get so caught up in your old life patterns that you lose focus on where you want to be.

You have to want more out of life; there comes a time when you have to do it. Make your dreams more significant than your fears. We all have concerns, and we all have goals. Don't let your fears stop you from dreaming of bigger and better things. We have to dig deep and find the courage.

As I close out this chapter, remember this. Go out and find your gift and embrace your failure. Continue to push through the dirt, and always surround yourself with like-minded individuals. Always dream more prominent than your fears; make friends with those who are just as hungry as you.

CHAPTER SIX

Motivation

Remember that staying focus is essential when trying to achieve anything in life. If you get to a point where all you are doing is struggling, it's time to do something about it. Stop complaining and take control of your life. We all are unique individuals; no two persons are alike. When you leap with faith, you have to believe that God will be with you every step of the way.

We have to say enough is enough. Set your requirements high and stick to it. We all have the ability to do whatever we want; you first have to believe that you can do it. No matter what problems you face in life or how difficult it may be, keep fighting. Stop holding on to those whom you have outgrown in life; there's a reason why you outgrown them.

Sometime you need to be around those who can positively motivate you. You have to learn that you can never lose what was never yours. If it doesn't belong to you stop holding on to it. Instead, go out and take what belongs to you and hold on to it tight. Occasionally you have to do it for yourself; it's not about doing it for someone else.

Only you can live your life. Nobody else can live it for you. Never lose sight of what you want out of life. Always be careful of those you trust. I want to ask you this; what are you willing to leave behind? Often we have to let go of something to get something better. Learn from that mistake, and don't repeat the mistake twice. Never let them lead you away from what God has in store for you.

Our first few steps are always the hardest. Once you take those first few steps, things get easier. Today is the day you start being a winner. It's better to start for you to start somewhere than not start at all. Why sit on the sideline; get up, get in the game, and play the game to win. Stop depending on everyone else.

Only you can control the outcome of your future. No one else can do it for you. No matter how hard it may get or what other people may say or think, believe in yourself and have faith in the abilities that are in you. All you can do in life is to try your best. Nothing else matters as long as you know you gave it you're all.

Let your thoughts be what keeps you motivated. With that said, always think big and motivate yourself to feel like a winner. While everyone else is sleeping, get up early, and be prepared. Nothing comes to a sleeper but a dream. Don't just dream about it; wake up and be about it. It's not always about being spot on about what you want.

It's more about the effort you put into getting to where you want to be. Suppose you want to see transformation put in the effort. Don't just show an attempt once a week; show effort daily. When you can do that, you will see the transformation take place. There's no reason why we can't live the life you dream about.

The greatest pleasure in life is going out and doing things everyone says you can't do. If you fail today, there's always tomorrow. We have to learn that it doesn't matter how low you fall in life. What matters is that you never gave up. If your determination is important failure can't slow you down. When you can change the level of your thinking, you can change the life you living.

We can talk about it all day. But if you not doing nothing about it, then you just wasting time. Don't get caught up in talking about your dreams with others. They too busy worrying about trying to reach their own. Don't get lost in someone else dream that you forget about yours. Another thing don't fail over something that could've been prevented.

Failure can't overtake you if you have the determination of a mustard seed. In life we will encounter many defeats. But what matters is how you react to defeat. When you have confidence in yourself, nothing else matters but your determination to do it.

What may seem impossible now will be your accomplishment of tomorrow. No matter how long it take you never stop reaching. Make your future work in your favor, believe in yourself, and have faith in your abilities. When you make it to where you want to be? Never regret the things in your past. Allow those things to be motivated to do better.

Learn from those mistakes and build an empire around them. Never wish and hope for what you want. Instead, work hard at it until you get it. The seed you plant now will slowly grow and blossom in the future. Get out of your comfort zone and allow yourself to grow.

When you can overcome challenges life will be more meaningful. Don't be like others who are just here to follow someone else's path. Instead, go out and make your path.

Always be the one who is making the path, not the one who is following the path. It's better to be the leader than a follower. Why pursue a route when you can create your own route.

One of our fundamental purposes in life is to be happy. Life is what we make of it. We only live once why not make the best out of it. The only impossible thing is the one you never tried or begin to do. Never have regrets. Instead get up and try again. When you fall rise up stronger let that be motivation to keep going.

Why make life complicated; we all have the opportunity to change the world. Life can be so simple; it's our way of thinking that makes it hard. We have to learn that humility is a part of living. Nothing is impossible; you have to work hard at getting it. Don't be one of those who get disappointed by something you were afraid to do. Be the one who wasn't afraid to take risks.

I tell you this if you able to think it then you can achieve it. Don't wait for change to come to you be the change. Never change to fit in with others. Instead be yourself, and the right people will come around. Make choices that will enable you to change your life; never make choices that will set you up for failure.

Everyday look for something positive to keep you motivated. Somedays you may have to look harder than other days. It doesn't matter where you come from and what you have done. The only thing that matters is that you change your ways. Once you can change you can get back on the right path. Remember, life will always test you.

Our mistakes are our opportunity to learn and become smarter, and not to make the same mistake twice. Today is the day you break free from that prison and take control of your life. Always push yourself to be better; don't ever give up when it gets hard. Don't depend on others to lead you; be willing to teach yourself, and others will walk with you. Get yourself motivated to be more than average.

If being excellent was easy to reach, the whole world would be perfect and filled with extraordinary people. Sometimes, you have to push hard to get by. Always believe in yourself because everyone else may not want you to be successful; you have to stay in tune with your goals. Remember that it's not about being the best; it's about not being the worst.

When you get up in the morning, get up with the mindset that you can. Wake up with the determination that you are going to conquer the world. That you will be a winner and not a loser. Don't allow yourself to get weakened by the barriers of the world; go into the world and challenge yourself to overcome whatever stands in your way.

Don't allow the things of this world to intimidate you. Instead let those things be what gives you strength. The best thing about proving everyone wrong is believing in yourself and succeeding. Never be afraid of where you going be fearful of going back where you came. In life, it doesn't matter where you have been.

When everyone else counts you out, believe in yourself, and stay humble. Having confidence in yourself is better than the spirit of a thousand individuals. Never make the mistake of being comfortable where you are. Always leave some room open to go above and beyond your limits. A champion believes in themselves when no one else does. Never do something to glorify men; do it because it's the right thing.

Don't allow your past lifestyle keep you captive let loose and bloom into something beautiful. If you want to be healthy learn how to think healthier. On days when it may seem cloudy, go out and make it shine. Let this be the day, the month, the year you take control. Being more assertive and braver starts now, not tomorrow.

The greatest thing you can ever do is believe in you. Not only that doing what you know is the right thing to do. If you is not too sure about it. Then more likely you shouldn't be doing it. Don't worry about others' success. The success of others doesn't define your success. Be willing to work hard at being the *best* of the *best.*

Sometimes, you have to do things you don't want to do until you can do what you want. Take your time, never rush the process; good things always take time. Don't wait for someone else to motivate you; go out and motivate yourself. We often get caught up doing what others want us to do and forget to do what we want. When you fail to stay focused life become a blur.

We all have the opportunity to do unlimited things. Nothing is impossible as long as we act accordingly. Don't let fear stop you from living, and don't let fear stop you from doing the impossible. Whatever you want in life will take hard work. Always be authentic in

what you do and be willing to chase your
dreams to the end of the earth.

CHAPTER SEVEN

Author Letter

To those of you returning home know that things will be fine. We all make mistakes as I've made many. Every day we make many decisions, and those decisions is what forms our future. I'm not here to judge you but encourage you to get past your mistakes and start over.

I hope you used your time to reflect on past mistakes and adjust for your future. Those changes should set the standard for your decision-making process going forward. Every time you decide to do right, you're creating a better future. I know deep down each of you are good people. You are people who made a mistake and want to get past those mistakes.

The choices we make not only affect us; they also affect those around us. The bad friendships you keep will only lead to destruction. That's why it is essential to surround yourself with people who want the best for you. I'm telling you this because I've been in your shoes; I know what it's like on the inside.

I know what the struggle is like when you in a place like that. I know what the experience is like coming home. Life hands each of us some real lemons and they are sour. We often don't control what happens to us, but we always have absolute control over how we react.

There comes a time in life when you have to say enough is enough. You have to decide how you want to be known. Today is the day you decide how you want to live the rest of your life. Start setting your goals today to get where you want to be later. Life is too short to continue to go down the wrong road.

How do you chose to live life? Now would be an excellent time to make that change. If you don't do it now, then when will you make the change? Making a break from the old and establishing the new takes courage, but you know we're all behind you. Those individuals will steer you in the right direction.

I want to remind you always to look up, no matter how hard life may be. Always look up when you are unsure what tomorrow will bring; those struggling with life, hold on to hope, for things will get better. But always remember, you hold the key to your destiny. Today, let's encourage one another to do better and be better; our past does not define our future.

When you think you have lost all hope and hit rock bottom remember the only way to go now is up. I hope the words I shared with you help you along the way. Remember that you can be whatever you want to be. Please continue to keep your head up and never give us. Be the change that will make a difference in the world.

ABOUT THE AUTHOR

Michael Davis is a former Paralegal and advocate he received his Associate degree in Paralegal in (2013). Michael is also the author of The Road to Reentry (2017) Michael is also a certified Life Coach. He has been a part of many different organizations, to name a few—the Reentry Advocacy Project, The National Federation of Paralegal Association, The Center for Economic and Social Justice, and The America Bar Association.

Notes